Contents

Backyard Bugs

Written by Josh Ryan

Many kinds of bugs
live in the garden.

They live in grass.
They live in flowers.
They live under leaves
and bark and rocks.

They feed on the plants
that grow in the garden.

3

Some backyard bugs are fliers.
They fly to find food
in the garden.
They fly away from danger
in the garden.

Honeybee

They fly to find a safe place
to lay their eggs in the garden.

Butterfly

Ladybird

Beetle

5

Some backyard bugs are leapers.
Grasshoppers and crickets
are good leapers.
They use their long, strong legs
to jump and hop in the garden.

Grasshopper

Cricket

Some backyard bugs are creepers.
Ants, caterpillars, and spiders
are good creepers.
They creep and crawl over leaves
and rocks in the garden.

Ant

Spider

Caterpillar

Some backyard bugs are tricksters.
They hide in the garden.
They try to look like
the things around them.

How many backyard bugs
can you find in your garden?

Wriggly Worms

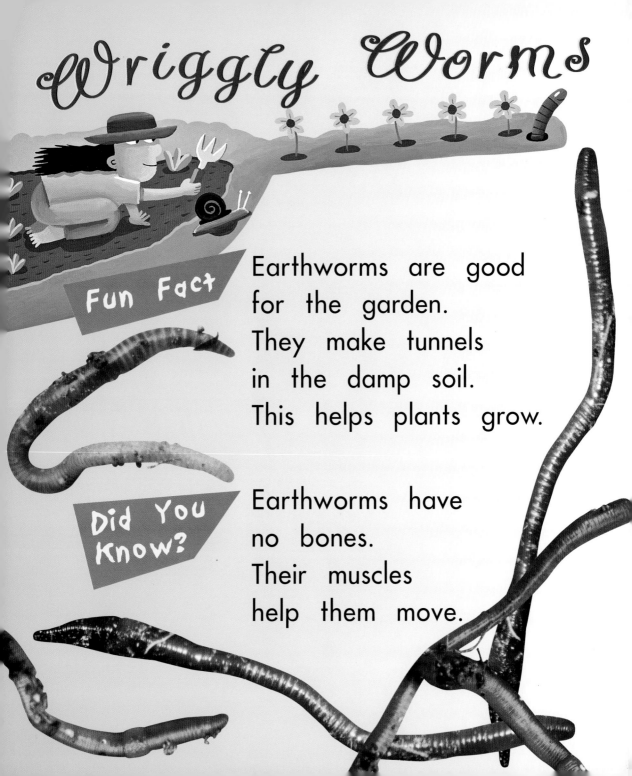

Fun Fact

Earthworms are good
for the garden.
They make tunnels
in the damp soil.
This helps plants grow.

Did You Know?

Earthworms have
no bones.
Their muscles
help them move.

The Worm

10

When the earth is turned in spring,
the worms are as fat as anything.
And birds come flying all around
to eat the worms from off the ground.

They like worms as much as I
like bread and milk and apple pie.
And once, when I was very young,
I put a worm right on my tongue.

I didn't like the taste a bit,
and so I didn't swallow it.
But, oh, it makes my mother squirm
because she *thinks* I ate that worm!

Ralph Bergengren

Garden

The Throw-Away Tree

Written by Lynette Evans   Photographed by Jeff Evans
Illustrated by Chelsea Evans

"This backyard is bare,"
said Grandpa.
"We need to plant a tree."

"Let's go to the plant
shop and look for
a tree," I said.

Grandpa's
bare garden.

16

So off we went.

Grandpa and I looked
at rows and rows of trees.
Some trees had red leaves.
Some trees had green leaves.
And some trees had
golden-yellow leaves.

At the
plant shop.

17

Grandpa and I
looked at big trees
and little trees.
We looked at
fruit trees and
flowering trees.

18

"I like this tree, Grandpa,"
I said.

"That tree's no good,"
said the woman
at the plant shop.
"It's a throw-away tree.
It's too little.
It's not growing well.
You should get
another tree."

"Can we please buy this
tree, Grandpa?" I said.
"We'll look after it.
It'll grow big and strong.
It'll look good in
our bare backyard."

"It's a throw-away tree,"
said the woman.
"You can have it
for free!"

19

We took our little
throw-away tree home.

We dug a big hole
in the backyard.

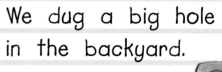

We put our little tree
in the hole. Then we put
lots of soil around it.

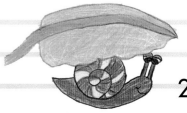

Grandpa's
garden
isn't so
bare now!

I gave our little
throw-away tree
a drink of water.

21

Every day, I talked to our little tree.
Every day, I sang to our little tree.
I even read stories to our little tree.

I was right!

Our little throw-away tree
grew and **grew** and **grew!**

23

The Apple Orchard

There are ten apples in every row of trees. Scarecrow Sam can tell how many apples grow on each tree by the number of apples on the corner trees. Can you?

Remember to count down and across!

25

The Girl Who Wished

An Old Story from China

Illustrated by Jingwen Wang and Xiangyi Mo

Once upon a time,
there was a girl who worked
in the garden of a beautiful palace.
Every day, the girl picked flowers
from the palace garden.

Every day, the girl took the flowers to a lady with a vase.

Every day, the lady put the flowers in the vase and took them to the empress.

The girl was happy
working in the garden.

But, one day, she said,
"*I* would like to put
the flowers in the vase.
I would like to take
the flowers
to the empress."

Now the girl
was not happy.
"I wish *I* was
the lady
with the vase!"
she said.

29

There was a *flash* of lightning.

There was a *crash* of thunder...

and the girl was the lady
with the vase!

For a while,
the girl was happy.
Every day, she put
the flowers in
the vase. Every day,
she took the flowers
to the empress.

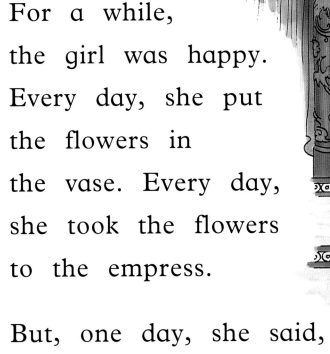

But, one day, she said,
"*I* would like
to be the empress."
Now the girl
was not happy.
"I wish *I* was
the empress!"
she said.

There was a *flash* of lightning.

There was a *crash* of thunder...

and the girl was the empress!

For a while, the girl
was happy. Every day,
a girl in the garden
picked the flowers.
Every day, a lady
put the flowers
in a vase for her.

But, one day, she said,
"*I* would like to pick
the flowers myself."
Now the girl
was not happy.
"I wish *I* was
the girl who picked
the flowers," she said.

There was a flash of lightning.

There was a crash of thunder...

and the girl was herself once more!

This time, the girl was happy.
She didn't make any more wishes.
She was happy to be herself
and pick flowers in the garden
for the empress.

Sow a Summer Garden

You Will Need:

1 Fill a tub with soil.

2 Design and label your garden.

3 Plant the seeds.

4 Water the seeds.

5 Decorate your garden and watch it GROW!

Gardening Boots

Written by Diane Foley
Illustrated by Helen Bacon

Grandpa Green
had a very old pair
of gardening boots
he liked to wear.

They were so old
that they let in the rain,
but the holes in the toes
let it out again.

Now Grandma Green
she made a face,
and said the boots
were a big disgrace.

Then, pointing
to the rubbish bin,
she told poor Grandpa
to put them in.

"No!" cried Grandpa.
"No, no, no.
I just can't let
my old boots go!"

Grandma had him
in a fix,
but then he saw
the potting mix.

40

He filled each boot
and added seeds.
He watered them
and pulled out weeds.

Now Grandma thinks
those gardening boots
look great filled up
with nice green shoots!

A TRUE STORY
The Butterfly

Written by Lynette Evans   Photographed by Jeff Evans
Illustrated by Hui-Yao Hsu

Grandma has a caterpillar tree in her garden. There are lots of little caterpillars on Grandma's tree.

Hospital

We counted
the little caterpillars.
We watched them
munch holes
in the leaves.
We watched them
grow long and fat.

43

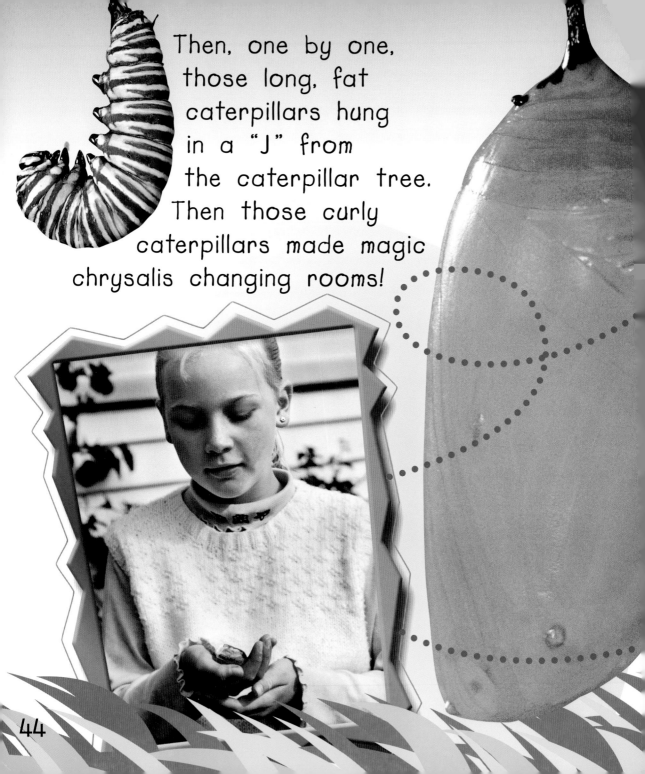

Then, one by one, those long, fat caterpillars hung in a "J" from the caterpillar tree. Then those curly caterpillars made magic chrysalis changing rooms!

44

But, one day,
a big storm came.
The wind blew hard.
It shook the caterpillar tree.
Ten chrysalises fell down.
We took them inside
and hung them from a shelf.

We watched and we waited.
Would the butterflies still come out?

45

Hooray!

The butterflies did come out.

We counted
four butterflies
with good wings.
We took them outside
and watched them
fly away.

We counted four butterflies
with crumpled wings.
They tried to fly,
but their crumpled wings
didn't work.
So we made
a butterfly hospital.

We gave the crumpled butterflies
a plate of fruit and flowers.
We gave the crumpled butterflies
a plate of honey water.

They ate and drank
with their long, black tongues.
They fluttered around
in the warm, bright sun.

Now Grandma feeds
the butterflies every day.
She puts them in the sun
when she goes to work.
She puts them outside
when she does the gardening.

She rounds them up
when it's time for bed.
(Sometimes Grandma's
little dog helps with
the butterfly round-up, too!)

And we have four new friends
to play with when we go over
to Grandma's place!

Letters That Go Together

fl flash, flowers   **th** then, there

Sounds I Know

- **ai**   again, rain
- **ace**   disgrace, face
- **ate**   plate

Endings I Know

- **ies**   butterfly, butterflies
- **s**   flower, flowers

Words I Know

day	I'll	our	was
every	it's	there	watched
fly	little	they	wish
grew	live	took	would